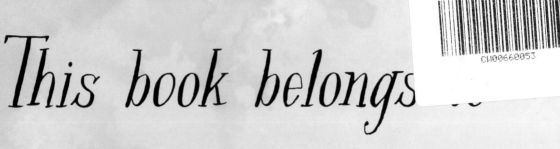

This book belongs to

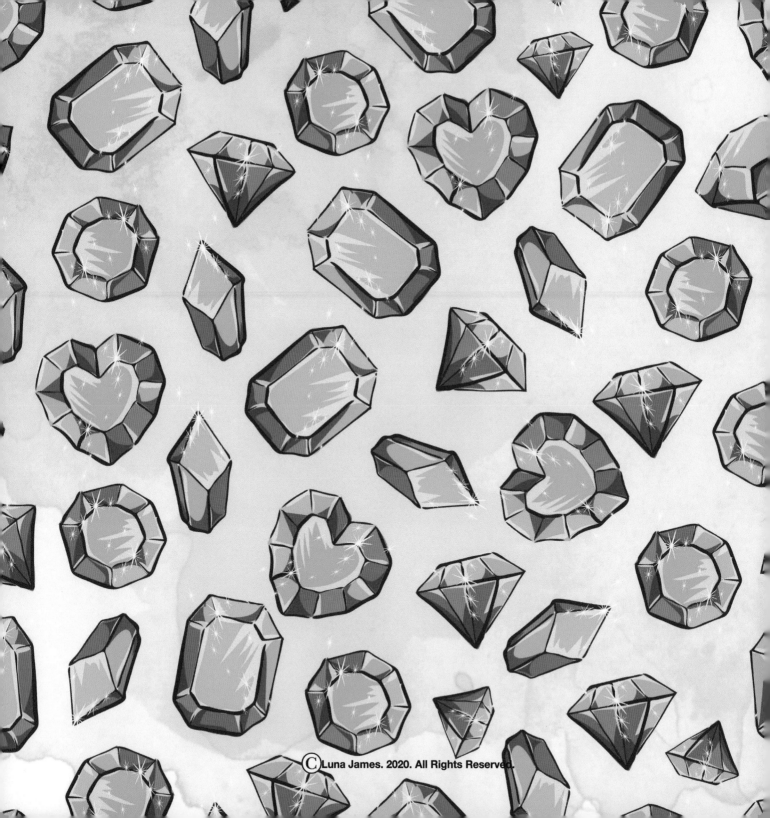

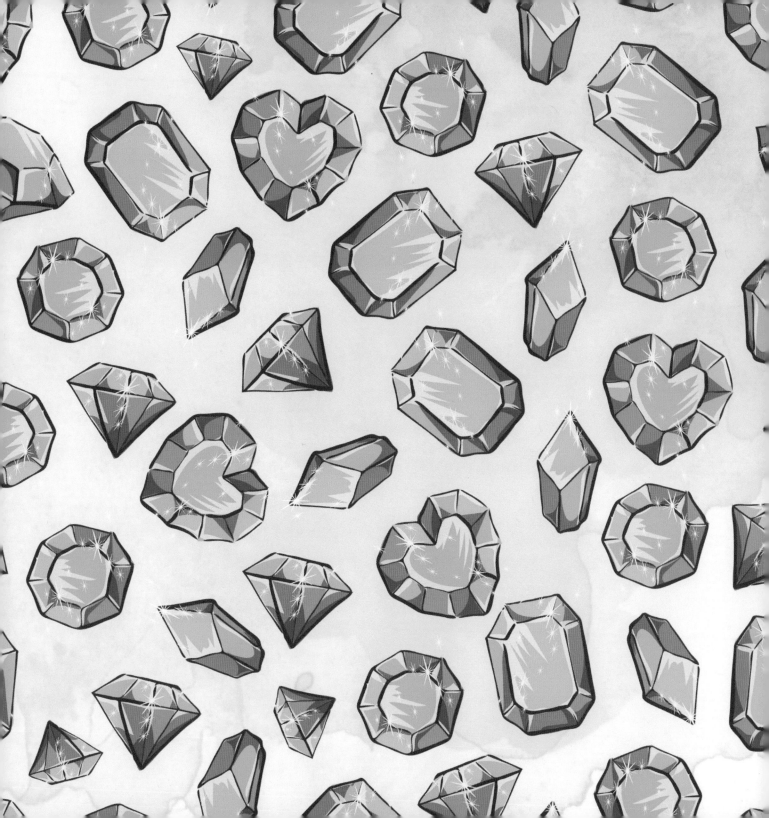

Deep in the green forest
live some leprechauns.

to be precise.

They are very unusual
creatures.

Most are sneaky and
very cheeky.

If you hear a

Do not fear; it's only the leprechauns making shoes.

They love their green
hats,
Green cupcakes and their
special green
brew.

Some can even play
the harp.

They have tiny little
dogs as pets.

Rumor has it that every leprechaun has a hidden pot of gold at the end of a rainbow.

Some say that
four-leaf clovers
are their weakness,
but it is yet to be
confirmed.

Either way, they are lucky little fellows.

If you are lucky enough to catch one on this fine St. Patrick's Day,

You will get three wishes, and best of all, you will be able to go to the annual super-secret Leprechaun St. Patrick's Day spectacular.

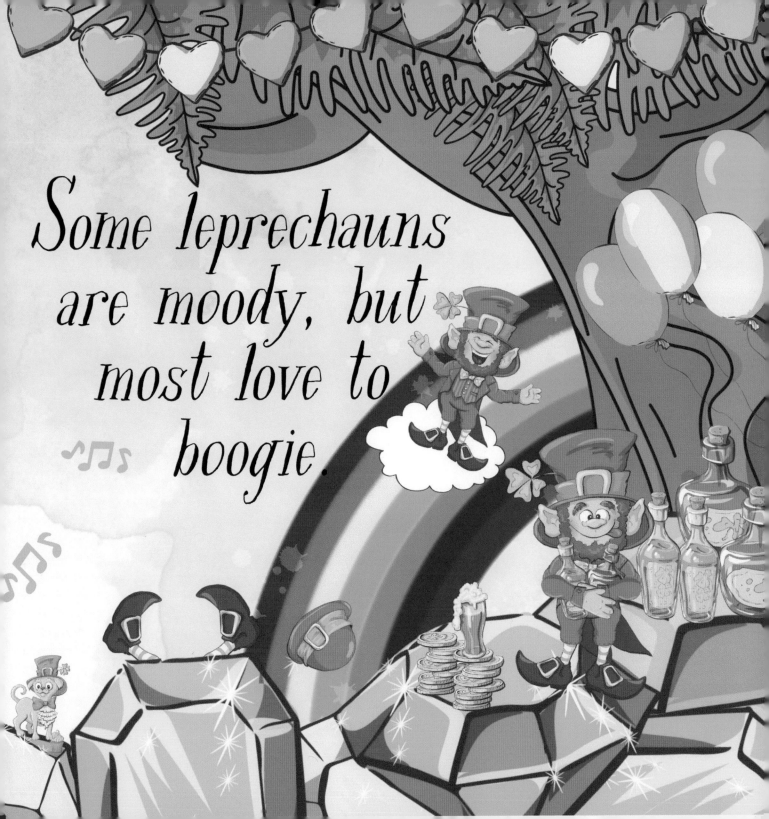

Some leprechauns are moody, but most love to boogie.

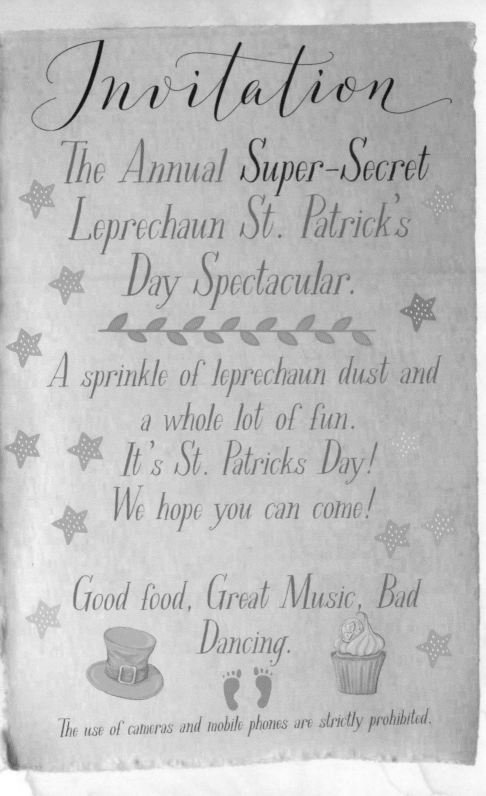

Invitation

The Annual Super-Secret Leprechaun St. Patrick's Day Spectacular.

A sprinkle of leprechaun dust and
a whole lot of fun.
It's St. Patricks Day!
We hope you can come!

Good food, Great Music, Bad Dancing.

The use of cameras and mobile phones are strictly prohibited.

Happy St. Patrick's Day!

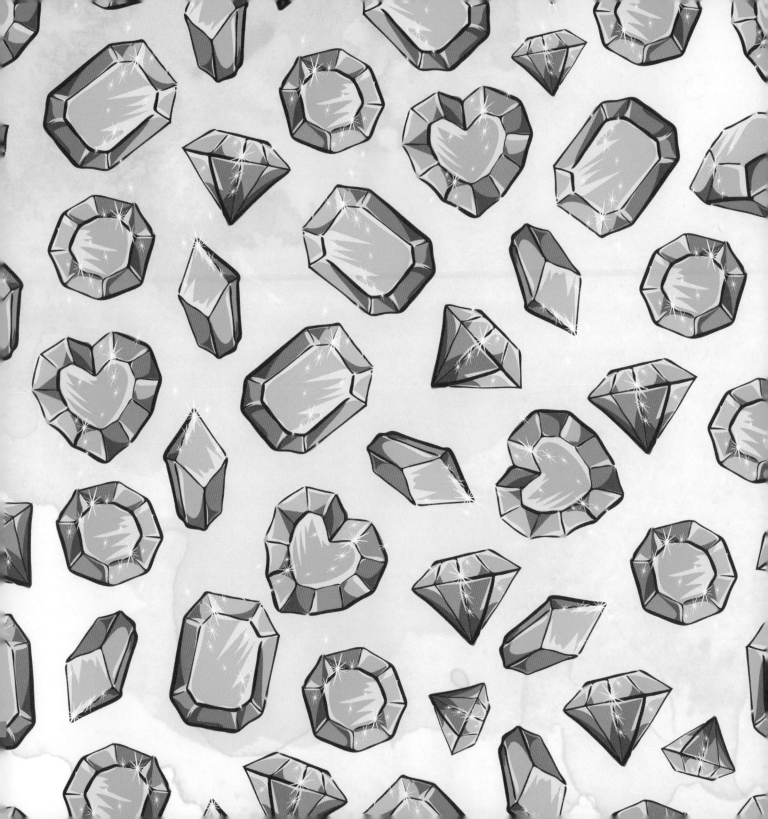

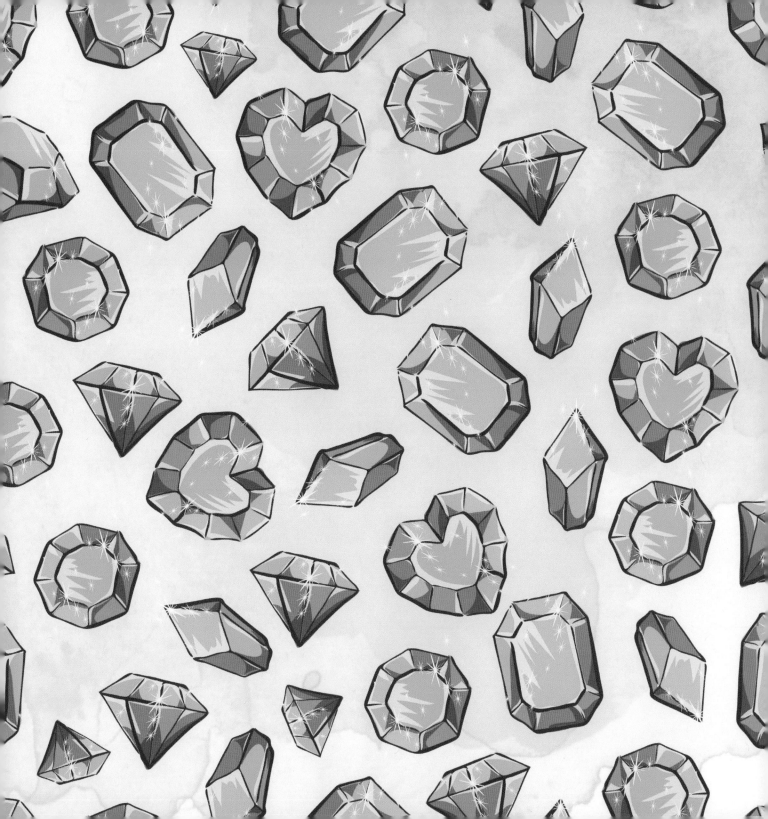

If you have enjoyed this book, please leave a review on Amazon.
It has a significant impact on independent creatives like myself.

Thank you so much!

Luna James

Printed in Great Britain
by Amazon

21093660R00022

Grammar

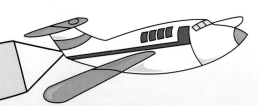
Writing sentences

This book belongs to:

Giving a child an analogy they can relate to has always been the key to Letterland's success. *Letterland Grammar* describes stories as towns; within those towns there are streets, or sentences. The words we see are the buildings, and just as buildings are modified, extended or developed, so words change with the addition of prefixes, suffixes and tenses. Punctuation is represented by road signs.

In *Letterland Grammar*, as your child reads, they are encouraged to think of their finger on the page as a car travelling along a street looking out for 'reading' signs along the way. Use the 'Little car' finger puppet to bring this idea to life!

Stop, look, listen!
Read through these sections with your child. It's important that the concept is introduced clearly first.

Get set
These are examples to work through together slowly. Give your child support and encouragement as they complete the activities.

Go!
Encourage your child to have a go at these activities on their own.

Contents of Activity Book 2

This *Letterland Grammar Activity Book* uses the analogy of buildings on a street to help children combine words to make sentences. It explains how conjunctions or joining words are a bit like bridges that connect words or phrases together.

Just as there are lots of different types of streets, so there are lots of different types of sentences. This activity book helps children to recognise the grammatical patterns of expanded noun phrases, statements, questions, exclamations and commands.

Stop, look, listen!

Imagine that the stories you read are like towns, made up of lots of interesting and different streets. Those streets are like the sentences in a story and the words in each sentence are like buildings.

There are words that act as little bridges to connect buildings or groups of buildings. These words are called '**conjunctions**' or joining words. One of the most common conjunctions we use is the word '**and**'.

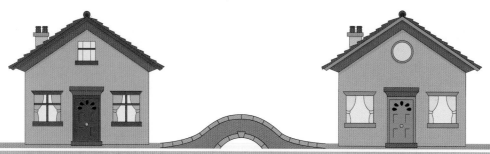

bucket and spade

salt and pepper

The word '**and**' can also be used to connect clauses or groups of words to make full sentences.

She took her scarf   and   her gloves.

He has a dog   and   two cats.

They went to the park   and   played on the swings.

Draw a line to connect each sentence start to the end that makes most sense. Notice how the conjunction '**and**' joins the two clauses together.

I'd like fish fingers   and   lettuces in her garden.

She grows tomatoes   and   began to read.

He cleaned his teeth   and   shut the door quietly.

The cat has soft fur   and   chips for dinner.

He picked up his book   and   broke her arm.

She fell off the swing   and   washed his face.

He tiptoed out of the house   and   a loud purr.

Write a sentence about what you did yesterday, using the conjunction '**and**' to join words or groups of words together, e.g: *I stayed at home **and** played with my cat.*

Get set...

Using the conjunction '**and**', join the two short sentences to make one long sentence. Check the full stops and capital letters are correct!

I went to the shops. I bought a new cap.

_____

We flew our kite. It went very high.

_____

The dog chased the cat. The cat ran up the tree.

_____

It was late. We were tired.

_____

Daniel put on his boots. He jumped in the puddles.

_____

You've got it! Let's go camping.

6

STICKER TIME!

The Harrison family are going camping.
They are packing everything they need. Use the stickers
to connect the words or phrases in these sentences.
See how useful the conjunction '**and**' is!

Go!

I'll water your plants, feed your cat [ ] keep an eye on the house while you're away.

I've packed the toothbrushes [ ] toothpaste [ ] remembered to put in my hairbrush too.

Hope you have a great time [ ] don't forget to send me a postcard.

I want to take all my cuddly toys [ ] my cars [ ] my puzzles.

Can you get the buckets [ ] spades from the shed [ ] the camping table [ ] chairs out of the garage?

I'm putting the plates, bowls [ ] cups into this box.

7

Just as there are lots of different types of bridges, so there are lots of different types of words that work as conjunctions, or joining words. Some bridges join groups of houses that are the same style. These are a bit like '**coordinating conjunctions**', which join words and phrases that are of equal importance in a sentence.

'**And**' is a coordinating conjunction.

I like drawing and painting.

The words '**so**', '**but**' and '**or**' are **coordinating conjunctions** too.

He was hungry so he ate an apple.

She likes cheese but she doesn't like pizza.

We could go swimming or bowling.

Circle the **conjunction** that best completes these sentences.

It was raining so / but / or they couldn't play outside.

Would you like an apple so / but / or a banana?

The dog was big so / but / or it was very gentle.

Sam has written about the journey to the campsite in his diary. Help him to choose the correct **conjunction** to join the parts of each sentence together. Make sure you use each one *at least once*.

and	but	so	or

Today we drove to the campsite. We were all very excited! I wanted to bring lots of toys _____ Dad said there wasn't room. The car boot was full _____ the tent had to go in the roof box. There wasn't room for the dinghy _____ we left that behind.

We had bags by our feet _____ our pillows next to us. Dad said we could go on the motorway _____ on country roads. He chose the country roads _____ I think the motorway would have been faster. We got stuck behind lots of tractors! It was a long journey _____ we played I-Spy. Evie felt sick _____ mum opened a window. We listened to music _____ sang loudly.

We got hungry _____ mum gave us some biscuits. There were chocolate ones _____ plain ones. I had a chocolate one _____ it melted. I got very messy.

Stop, look, listen!

Some bridges join groups of houses that are different styles together. In the same way, '**subordinating conjunctions**' join together words and groups of words which add extra meaning, but are less important than the rest of the sentence.

The words '**when**', '**if**', '**that**', and '**because**' are **subordinating conjunctions**.

He was tired because he went to bed late.

She will go back to school when she is feeling better.

They get extra time to play if they finish their work.

The dog ate the food that the child dropped.

Get set...

Circle the **conjunction** that best completes these sentences.

You don't have to go when / if / that / because you don't want to.

You can play outside when / if / that / because you have tidied your room.

She likes the rabbit when / if / that / because is in this hutch.

We got wet when / if / that / because it started raining.

Camping fun!

Evie has written a postcard to her friend, Amy. Use the stickers to put in the **conjunctions** that join the parts of each sentence together.

Go!

| when | if | that | because |

Dear Amy

We're having a great time camping.

Yesterday we went to the beach ⬚ it was sooooo hot!

We built a sandcastle ⬚ was a-maz-ing! Dad says we can go back to the beach tomorrow ⬚ the weather is still nice.

Today we're going to visit a castle, ⬚ everybody is ready. Sam takes ages to get dressed!

I love sleeping in the tent. Only problem is I keep rolling off my airbed ⬚ our tent is on a slope. Mum says it might be better ⬚ I sleep the other way round. I'm going to try that tonight.

Will tell you all about the rest of my holiday ⬚ I get back. Miss you.

From Evie

11

So far we've looked at 'when', 'if', 'that' and 'because', but there are lots of other words that can be **subordinating conjunctions**.

Here are some more examples:

after until before when
once where since than

Choose a **subordinating conjunction** from the box above to join the two parts of each sentence together. You may notice that *more than one* of the conjunctions would make sense. If that's the case, you choose the one you like the best.

Dad will clean the tent _____ packing it away.

Sam jumped up _____ the campfire crackled.

Sam ran faster _____ his sister.

Keep your seatbelt on _____ the car is switched off.

Clean your teeth _____ you go to sleep.

Toothpaste

Write a sentence of your own, using a **subordinating conjunction**.

_____

_____

Just as a street has different types of buildings on it, so a sentence is made up of different types of words. Each type of word has its own job to do in the sentence.

Nouns are the words that name things such as people, places or objects.

The bird built a nest.

Circle the **nouns** in these sentences.

Jake walked to school.

The dog barked at the postman.

Shut the door, please.

Tom fell off the wall.

Draw a line to match the **noun** with its picture.

car

box

fish

garden

Stop, look, listen!

Imagine a **noun** is like a house. A **noun phrase** is like the pathway leading up to that house or the bits of land around it. Some buildings have a little bit of land around them and some have lots, so **noun phrases** can be short or long.

A simple **noun phrase** describes the noun.

An **expanded noun phrase** gives more information about the noun.

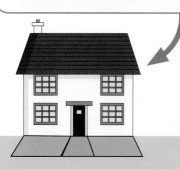

the white house → the white house with the lovely garden

his coat → his winter coat

Get set...

Tick the box to show whether the phrases below are simple

noun phrases 🏠 or **expanded noun phrases**. 🏡

a big, red balloon

the huge tree that towered above our house

brightly coloured flags that danced in the wind

crying baby

the calm sea

gigantic waves that crashed against the shore

The steps below show how you can write an **expanded noun phrase**.

1. Choose a **noun**.

dog	giant	house	robot

Example: dog

2. Choose a description.

old	black	spooky	rusty	huge	grumpy	happy

Example: black

3. Put them together to create a simple **noun phrase**.

Example: the black dog

4. Now expand your simple **noun phrase** by adding more description.

where nobody lives	that shouts at the top of his voice
with the wagging tail	that squeaks when it moves
that moves really fast	with the broken window

Example: the black dog with the wagging tail

Use the ideas above to write *three* **expanded noun phrases**.

_____

_____

_____

Here are some photographs of the Harrison family camping holiday.
Write a **noun phrase** for each of these pictures.

tent

sandcastle

beach

crab

shell

dolphin

Streets have different functions defined by the buildings that are on them. Residential streets are full of houses and flats; shopping streets have shops and cafes; business areas have offices.

Just as streets have different functions, so do sentences. Here are four types of sentences that each have a particular job to do.

A **statement** simply tells you something. I love dancing. She climbed up the tree.	An **exclamation** expresses a strong feeling.* Hooray! I did it! 
A **question** is asking something. Where are you going? Can I have one of those?	A **command** tells you to do something. Shut the door. Tell him to come here.

*The English National Curriculum at Key Stage 1 defines an exclamation as a sentence starting with **what** or **how** and including a verb, for example: What a good friend you are! How kind of you to think of me! However, an exclamation mark can have wider usage.*

Get set...

Draw a line to match each sentence to the correct sentence type.

Why did you do that?   statement

Go away.   question

Ella jumped in.   exclamation

How exciting!   command

Use the stickers to show whether these sentences are **statements**, **questions**, **exclamations** or **commands**.

STICKER TIME!

Camping fun

How sad we were when the holiday ended!

What a great time we had!

The dolphin swam close to our boat.

Watch out!

Are you hungry?

My favourite colour is red.

Can we go to the park?

Walk quietly.

When did it happen?

Put your books away.

Get set...

You can turn **statements** into **questions** and **questions** into **statements**.

Statement

We are late.

Question

Are we late?

Write these **statements** as **questions**.

Statements   **Questions**

It is raining.   ⟶   _____

Apples are good for you.   ⟶   _____

The window is open.   ⟶   _____

Write these **questions** as **statements**.

Statements   **Questions**

_____   ⟵   Has she gone?

_____   ⟵   Have you got a pen?

_____   ⟵   Can your dad drive a car?

You can turn **questions** into **commands** too.

Question   **Command**

Can you take the dog for a walk? ⟷ Take the dog for a walk.

Turn these **questions** into **commands**.

Questions   **Commands**

Can you complete your   ⟶   _____

homework by tomorrow?

Could you walk quietly please? ⟶   _____

Can you shut the door?   ⟶   _____

Write two **questions** to ask Dad.

1. _____

2. _____

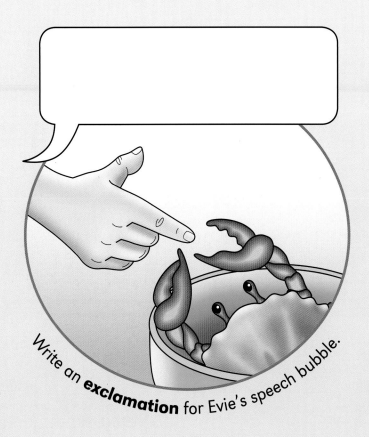

Write an **exclamation** for Evie's speech bubble.

What **command** is Mum giving Sam?

Write two **statements** about the picture.

1. _____

2. _____

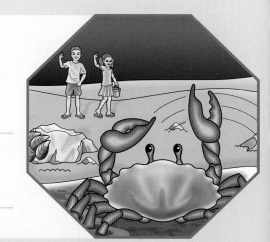

The holiday is over and the Harrison family are getting ready to go home.

I'm sad that our holiday is over.

Where did you put the water bottles?

What a great time we've had!

Put this rubbish in the bin.

Who is asking a **question**? _____

Who is giving a **command**? _____

Who is shouting an **exclamation**? _____

Who is making a **statement**? _____

Fill in the empty speech bubbles with a
statement, **question**, **exclamation** or **command** of your choice.
Remember to use the correct punctuation mark.

Grammar challenge

Can you use what you've learnt in this activity book in your own writing?
Have a go at these challenges and see how well you do.

Challenge 1
Imagine you are going camping with the Harrison family. Write a list of the things you would take. Write them in pairs. This is a great chance to practise using the **conjunction** 'and'.

Things to take camping

sunglasses and sun hat

How well did you do?
Underline all of the 'and' **conjunctions** in your list. Give yourself one point for every 'and' you included.

Points scored on Challenge 1:

Challenge 2
Imagine you've had a few days camping and you're writing all about it in your diary. What would you write? This is a great chance to practise using **coordinating and subordinating conjunctions**. You can use some **expanded noun phrases** too.

How well did you do?
Underline all of the **conjunctions** you used in your diary entry. Give yourself one point for each conjunction. Did you write an **expanded noun phrase** too? Give yourself five points for each expanded noun phrase you wrote.

Points scored on Challenge 2:

Challenge 3

Write one **statement**, **question**, **exclamation** and **command** that you might have used while you were camping with the Harrisons. This is a great chance to practise these different **sentence types**. Don't forget to use the correct punctuation mark.

Statement: _____

Question: _____

Exclamation: _____

Command: _____

How well did you do?
Did you use the correct punctuation mark for each type of sentence? If so give yourself one point for each sentence.

Points scored on Challenge 1:

Add up your scores

Points scored on Challenge 1:

Points scored on Challenge 2:

Points scored on Challenge 3:

Total Grammar challenge score:

Well done!
Are you pleased with your score?

Writing sentences

Give yourself a smiley face sticker for each section of this book you complete. Look out for the words, phrases and sentence types you've learnt about in this book when you read. Use them when you write too.

My name is:

I can...

- join phrases using the **conjunction** 'and'.

- use some other **coordinating conjunctions** in my writing.

- use **subordinating conjunctions** in my writing.

- recognise where some **coordinating and subordinating conjunctions** have been used in other pieces of writing.

- recognise a **noun**.

- recognise a **simple noun phrase**.

- recognise an **expanded noun phrase**.

- use **simple and expanded noun phrases** in my writing.

- understand that sentences have different functions.

- identify sentences as a **statement**, **question**, **exclamation** or **command**.

- use **statements**, **questions**, **exclamations** or **commands** in my writing.

24